Sad Day, Happy Day!
The Story of Peter and Dorcas

We are grateful to the following team of authors for their contributions to *God Loves Me*, a Bible story program for young children. This Bible story, one of a series of fifty-two, was written by Patricia L. Nederveld, managing editor for CRC Publications. Suggestions for using this book were developed by Sherry Ten Clay, training coordinator for CRC Publications and freelance author from Albuquerque, New Mexico. Yvonne Van Ee, an early childhood educator, served as project consultant and wrote *God Loves Me,* the program guide that accompanies this series of Bible storybooks.

Nederveld has served as a consultant to Title I early childhood programs in Colorado. She has extensive experience as a writer, teacher, and consultant for federally funded preschool, kindergarten, and early childhood programs in Colorado, Texas, Michigan, Florida, Missouri, and Washington, using the *High/Scope* Education Research Foundation curriculum. In addition to writing the *Bible Footprints* church curriculum for four- and five-year-olds, Nederveld edited the revised *Threes* curriculum and the first edition of preschool through second grade materials for the *LiFE* curriculum, all published by CRC Publications.

Ten Clay taught preschool for ten years in public schools in California, Missouri, and North Carolina and served as a Title IV preschool teacher consultant in Kansas City. For over twenty-five years she has served as a church preschool leader and also as a MOPS (Mothers of Preschoolers) volunteer. Ten Clay is coauthor of the preschool-kindergarten materials of the *LiFE* curriculum published by CRC Publications.

Van Ee is a professor and early childhood program advisor in the Education Department at Calvin College, Grand Rapids, Michigan. She has served as curriculum author and consultant for Christian Schools International and wrote the original *Story Hour* organization manual and curriculum materials for fours and fives.

Photo on page 5: Ken Fisher/Tony Stone Images; photo on page 20: SuperStock.

Library of Congress Cataloging-in-Publication Data

Nederveld, Patricia L., 1944-
     Sad day, happy day: the story of Peter and Dorcas/Patricia L. Nederveld.
       p. cm. — (God loves me; bk. 47)
     Summary: A rhyming retelling of the Bible story of a good woman
named Dorcas and how Peter's prayers raised her from the dead.
Includes follow-up activities.
   ISBN 1-56212-316-5
   1. Dorcas (Biblical figure)—Juvenile literature. 2. Peter, the
Apostle, Saint—Juvenile literature. [1. Dorcas (Biblical figure).
2. Peter, the Apostle, Saint. 3. Bible stories—N.T.] I. Title.
II. Series: Nederveld, Patricia L., 1944- God loves me; bk. 47.
BS2452.D67N43 1998
226.6'09505—dc21
                                   98-18517
                                    CIP
                                    AC

10 9 8 7 6 5 4 3 2 1

Sad Day, Happy Day!
The Story of Peter and Dorcas

PATRICIA L. NEDERVELD

ILLUSTRATIONS BY PAUL STOUB

CRC Publications
Grand Rapids, Michigan

This is a story from God's book, the Bible.

It's for *say name(s) of your child(ren).* It's for me too!

Acts 9:36-43

Dorcas loved to sew things—
then give them all away.
Shirts and skirts and dresses—
something lovely every day.

" Thank you for your goodness—dear Dorcas, we love you.
We can see that you love Jesus—it shows in all you do!"

But one day something happened that made her friends so sad. Kind Dorcas put her things away for she was feeling bad.

She climbed in bed and lay there. Friends gathered 'round and cried. But instead of feeling better, she grew worse— and then she died.

"We must hurry and tell Peter— he'll know just what to do." And when they found him, Peter said, "Okay, I'll go with you."

" **J**ust look what Dorcas made for us!"
friends gathered 'round to say.

But Peter sent them all outside,
then went inside to pray.

And taking Dorcas by the hand, he said, "Get up, my friend." She looked at him, she sat up straight, she was alive again!

17

Then sadness turned to gladness
as friends began to say,

"Our God made Dorcas live again!
Praise God! O happy day!"

wonder if you know that God helps you when you're sad . . .

Dear God, thank you for loving us. Thank you for helping us when we're feeling sad. Amen.

Suggestions for Follow-up

Opening

Welcome each little one with a smile and soft touch. Thank them for coming, and let the children know how happy you are to see them.

As you gather the children around you, pass around a hand mirror, and invite each child to look at the face in the mirror. Then pass the mirror around for another turn, and encourage your little ones to make happy or sad faces in the mirror. Thank God for loving us on sad days and happy days.

Learning Through Play

Learning through play is the best way! The following activity suggestions are meant to help you provide props and experiences that will invite the children to play their way into the Scripture story and its simple truth. Try to provide plenty of time for the children to choose their own activities and to play individually. Use group activities sparingly—little ones learn most comfortably with a minimum of structure.

1. Set out a few dress-up clothes and a full-length mirror, and invite your little ones to act out today's story. You can use a mat or blanket for a bed. You might want to play the part of Dorcas and hand out clothing to the children. Older children will be able to mimic your simple sentences and actions. Let them take turns helping Dorcas off the bed, and marvel with them that God made Dorcas live again!

2. Copy the sewing card (see Pattern T, *God Loves Me* program guide) on bright colored cardstock. For younger children, punch a row of four or five holes about 1" (2.5 cm) apart along one side of the card as shown. For older children, punch holes all around the card. Create a needle by wrapping the end of a length of yarn with a small piece of masking tape (or dip the end in white glue, and allow it to dry). Thread the yarn through the first hole, and tape the end to the back side of the card. Show your little ones how to thread the yarn through the holes, and talk about how Dorcas sewed clothes and gave them away.

3. Provide large pasta tubes and 12" (30 cm) lengths of yarn. Tie one end of the yarn through a pasta tube and knot it. Cover the other end of the yarn with a small piece of masking tape to make a needle. Show the children how to slip the yarn through the pasta tube to form a chain. Provide 3" (8 cm) sad/happy face circles to slip on the needle end of the chain, and tie a knot to form a hanger. (Older children may like to draw their own sad/happy faces.) Remind your little ones that God cares about us when we're feeling sad and when we're feeling happy.

4. Cut 6" (15 cm) squares of fabric of different textures and colors. Invite the children to touch the fabrics and find the ones that are soft, smooth, bumpy, scratchy. Encourage them to rub the fabric against their cheeks or on their arms and to arrange the squares to make pretty designs. Wonder if Dorcas might have made a shirt or dress from a certain color or

pattern. Older children might imagine what fabric they would have liked Dorcas to choose for them. Talk about how kind and loving Dorcas was. Her friends knew that she loved Jesus!

5. Tape squares of coarse-textured fabric like burlap or corduroy under a sheet of paper. Show your little ones how to rub the side of a crayon across the paper to make a textured design. Ask the children to tell you what Dorcas did and how her friends felt when she helped them, when she died, and when God made her live again.

Closing

Sing one or more of these stanzas of "God Is So Good" (Songs Section, *God Loves Me* program guide) as children mimic your actions:

> *God is so good* . . . (point up)
> *He cares for me* . . . (point to self)
> *God answers prayer* . . . (fold hands)
> *I praise his name* . . . (lift hands high)
> —Words: traditional

At Home

Your little one will sense happy moments and sad moments throughout the day. Make a sign together to hang on a doorknob or refrigerator. You might draw a simple circle with a happy face on one side and a sad face on the other. On each side write God Cares for Me. Whenever you turn the sign over, remind each other that God loves you when you're feeling sad and when you're feeling happy. Spend some time bringing happiness to others too. You might collect clothing your family no longer needs. Let your little one help you wash, dry, fold, and pack the clothes. If possible, go together to deliver the clothes to a shelter or needy family. Help your child express thanks that God takes care of your family and that you can help others.

Old Testament Stories

Blue and Green and Purple Too! *The Story of God's Colorful World*

It's a Noisy Place! *The Story of the First Creatures*

Adam and Eve *The Story of the First Man and Woman*

Take Good Care of My World! *The Story of Adam and Eve in the Garden*

A Very Sad Day *The Story of Adam and Eve's Disobedience*

A Rainy, Rainy Day *The Story of Noah*

Count the Stars! *The Story of God's Promise to Abraham and Sarah*

A Girl Named Rebekah *The Story of God's Answer to Abraham*

Two Coats for Joseph *The Story of Young Joseph*

Plenty to Eat *The Story of Joseph and His Brothers*

Safe in a Basket *The Story of Baby Moses*

I'll Do It! *The Story of Moses and the Burning Bush*

Safe at Last! *The Story of Moses and the Red Sea*

What Is It? *The Story of Manna in the Desert*

A Tall Wall *The Story of Jericho*

A Baby for Hannah *The Story of an Answered Prayer*

Samuel! Samuel! *The Story of God's Call to Samuel*

Lions and Bears! *The Story of David the Shepherd Boy*

David and the Giant *The Story of David and Goliath*

A Little Jar of Oil *The Story of Elisha and the Widow*

One, Two, Three, Four, Five, Six, Seven! *The Story of Elisha and Naaman*

A Big Fish Story *The Story of Jonah*

Lions, Lions! *The Story of Daniel*

New Testament Stories

Jesus Is Born! *The Story of Christmas*

Good News! *The Story of the Shepherds*

An Amazing Star! *The Story of the Wise Men*

Waiting, Waiting, Waiting! *The Story of Simeon and Anna*

Who Is This Child? *The Story of Jesus in the Temple*

Follow Me! *The Story of Jesus and His Twelve Helpers*

The Greatest Gift *The Story of Jesus and the Woman at the Well*

A Father's Wish *The Story of Jesus and a Little Boy*

Just Believe! *The Story of Jesus and a Little Girl*

Get Up and Walk! *The Story of Jesus and a Man Who Couldn't Walk*

A Little Lunch *The Story of Jesus and a Hungry Crowd*

A Scary Storm *The Story of Jesus and a Stormy Sea*

Thank You, Jesus! *The Story of Jesus and One Thankful Man*

A Wonderful Sight! *The Story of Jesus and a Man Who Couldn't See*

A Better Thing to Do *The Story of Jesus and Mary and Martha*

A Lost Lamb *The Story of the Good Shepherd*

Come to Me! *The Story of Jesus and the Children*

Have a Great Day! *The Story of Jesus and Zacchaeus*

I Love You, Jesus! *The Story of Mary's Gift to Jesus*

Hosanna! *The Story of Palm Sunday*

The Best Day Ever! *The Story of Easter*

Goodbye—for Now *The Story of Jesus' Return to Heaven*

A Prayer for Peter *The Story of Peter in Prison*

Sad Day, Happy Day! *The Story of Peter and Dorcas*

A New Friend *The Story of Paul's Conversion*

Over the Wall *The Story of Paul's Escape in a Basket*

A Song in the Night *The Story of Paul and Silas in Prison*

A Ride in the Night *The Story of Paul's Escape on Horseback*

The Shipwreck *The Story of Paul's Rescue at Sea*

Holiday Stories

Selected stories from the New Testament to help you celebrate the Christian year

Jesus Is Born! *The Story of Christmas*

Good News! *The Story of the Shepherds*

An Amazing Star! *The Story of the Wise Men*

Hosanna! *The Story of Palm Sunday*

The Best Day Ever! *The Story of Easter*

Goodbye—for Now *The Story of Jesus' Return to Heaven*

These fifty-two books are the heart of *God Loves Me,* a Bible story program designed for young children. Individual books (or the entire set) and the accompanying program guide *God Loves Me* are available from CRC Publications (1-800-333-8300).